THIS JOURNAL BELONGS TO:

____

Printed in Great Britain
by Amazon

41947800R00119